How Do We Use Forms of Energy?

 HOUGHTON MIFFLIN HARCOURT

PHOTOGRAPHY CREDITS: COVER ©JFB/Stone+/Getty Images; 3 (b) ©Jupiterimages/Polka Dot/Alamy; 4 (b) ©Grady Coppell/Getty Images; 5 (bg) ©JFB/Stone+/Getty Images; 6 (b) ©Zuma Wire Service/Alamy Images; 7 (t) ©Corbis; 8 (b) ©David Frazier/Corbis; 10 (b) ©Jupiterimages/Getty Images; 11 (t) ©Westend61/Getty Images; 13 (t) ©Hemera Technologies/Getty Images; 17 (t) ©Stockdisc/Getty Images; 18 (b) ©GIPhotoStock/Science Source/Photo Researchers, Inc.; 19 (l) ©Jose Luis Pelaez Inc./Blend Images/age fotostock; 19 (r) ©Stockbyte/Getty Images; 20 (b) ©Cheyenne Glasgow/Flikr/Getty Images; 21 (t) ©Katharine Andriotis Photography, LLC /Alamy Images

Printed in Mexico

ISBN: 978-0-544-07304-3

4 5 6 7 8 9 10 0908 21 20 19 18 17 16

4500608014   A B C D E F G

Be an Active Reader!

 **Look for each word in yellow along with its meaning.**

energy	chemical energy	conduction
potential energy	heat	convection
kinetic energy	thermal energy	radiation
mechanical energy	conductor	
electrical energy	insulator	

 Underlined sentences answer the questions.

What is energy?

What are the different forms of energy?

What causes sound?

What causes light?

Where does electrical energy come from?

What happens when fuels release chemicals?

What is heat?

How can energy change form?

How do objects react to heat?

How are conductors and insulators different?

How does an electric cord work?

How does heat move and change matter?

How do convection and radiation work?

What is energy?

Look around your classroom. Energy is all around you. Energy is the reason the lights are on. Energy is the reason the building stays warm or cool. Energy is necessary for computers to work. You use energy, too!

You use energy in everything you do. You use energy when you write. You use energy when you walk, run, or play a game. Even talking takes energy! But what is energy? Energy is the ability to cause change in matter. Any type of movement is a change. So, everything that moves has energy.

The boy uses energy to throw a ball.

What are the different forms of energy?

Have you ever dived into a pool? You put your arms up. You bend your knees. You push your feet off the board. You glide into the water.

It takes energy to dive. When you stand, energy is stored inside your body. The energy is waiting to be used. This is stored energy, or potential energy. Potential energy is the energy something has because of its position or condition.

When you push off and dive into the water, you are using another form of energy. This is kinetic energy. Kinetic energy is the energy of motion. You use kinetic energy when you dive, swim, and come out of the pool.

The ball has potential energy. The energy is stored. When the ball falls, it will have kinetic energy, or motion.

This diver dives off a platform. The diver has more potential energy at the top of the platform than at the bottom.

A diver stands on the edge of a platform. The diver has potential energy. Then the diver moves off the platform. The stored energy becomes kinetic energy. Potential and kinetic energy together are called mechanical energy.

When the diver moves off the platform, there is less potential energy. That's because the energy is now kinetic energy. The kinetic energy becomes greater as the diver moves toward the water. The total amount of mechanical energy is a combination of the potential energy and the kinetic energy.

What causes sound?

Walk in a dog park. What do you hear? You hear barking, of course! Did you know that the sound happens because of energy?

Sound is made when something vibrates, or moves back and forth. Pluck a guitar string. Notice that the string vibrates. The vibrations, or movements, make sound waves. The sound waves move through the air. Then the sound waves reach our ears, and we hear the music.

Loud sounds have more energy than quiet sounds do. Larger vibrations occur when sounds are loud. Pitch tells how high or low a sound is. A drum makes a low-pitched sound. A flute makes a high-pitched sound.

Imagine what a group of barking dogs sounds like. Is it a loud or quiet sound?

You can see light in this photograph. What two forms of energy produce the light?

What causes light?

Light is a form of energy. Light is produced by the sun. Sunlight moves through space to reach Earth. Plants use the light from the sun to make their food.

Electricity also produces light. Electricity brings light into our homes and other places. It also brings light to outdoor spaces at night. Ball games and carnivals can happen at night because of electricity. Where else can you see lights at night?

Where does electrical energy come from?

Electricity is electrical energy. Electrical energy is energy that comes from an electric circuit. Many things in your home, such as the TV, get energy from electricity. In most places, electrical energy comes from places called energy-generating stations. There, coal or natural gas is burned to produce electricity. In some places, wind energy is used to produce electricity. Energy from the sun is also used.

Did you ever lose electricity where you live? Your home had no light or heat. Lamps wouldn't turn on, and you couldn't use the microwave. You realized how important electricity is in your life. You understood that we all rely on electricity for many essential things.

Look at the view of the city at night. What do you notice about the buildings?

What happens when fuels release chemicals?

Fuel is a source of energy. Some types of fuels are coal, oil, gas, and wood. Energy-generating stations burn fuel. The burning causes a chemical reaction that produces heat energy. This is chemical energy, or energy that is released by chemical change. Chemical energy changes into other forms of energy.

You should eat a healthy breakfast every day. That's because food is our fuel. It gives us the energy we need to live. We are fueled by chemical energy!

Batteries in a flashlight store chemical energy. When you turn the switch, a chemical change happens. This chemical change causes a flow of electrical energy that causes the light to shine. Chemical energy is converted to light.

You need batteries for some toys to work. Batteries store chemical energy.

What is heat?

Heat is the transfer of kinetic energy from one object to another. It is the energy that moves between objects of different temperatures. Thermal energy is energy that is created by heat.

Picture yourself standing near a campfire. You feel the heat from the fire. It is a warm feeling. That's because you are getting heat energy. Heat moves from warmer things to cooler things.

To boil water, you place a pot of water on the stove. Heat moves from the burner to the pot. Then the heat moves from the pot to the water. The heat continues to move from hotter to cooler places.

This fireplace helps heat this home. The burning logs have heat energy. This heat moves to the cooler air in the room.

Erupting volcanoes are very hot. They can reach 1,250 °C or 2,000 °F.

Temperature measures how hot or cold something is. We use a tool called a thermometer to measure heat. Fahrenheit and Celsius are two scales for measuring heat. On the Fahrenheit scale, water boils at 212 °F and freezes at 32 °F. On the Celsius scale, water boils at 100 °C and freezes at 0 °C.

In winter, temperatures may fall below freezing. People have to wear warm clothing. Many animals have thick fur to help keep them warm. In Antarctica, temperatures can be well below 0 °C. They can be as low as –60 °C! The penguins living there stand very close together. This way, they can share the heat from their bodies.

How can energy change form?

You have learned about forms of energy. Energy can change from one form to another. For example, jump up and down. Stored energy inside you changes to kinetic energy when you move.

Now try to picture logs burning in a fireplace. What do you see when you look at them? What do you feel when you stand near them? The logs contain chemical energy. When logs burn, chemical energy changes to heat energy. It also changes to light.

Rub your hands together. Do they feel warm? Do you know why? It's because kinetic energy changes to heat energy.

The alarm clock's batteries have chemical energy. The alarm goes off! Chemical energy changes to electrical energy. Then electrical energy changes to sound energy!

Here are more ways that energy changes form.

- Turn on a light switch. Electrical energy changes to light energy. The light goes on.
- Turn on a radio and you hear music. Electrical energy changes to sound energy.
- Kick a ball to your teammate. Chemical energy in your body changes to movement. That is kinetic energy.
- Sit down at a piano. You have potential energy. Now begin to play music. Potential energy changes to kinetic energy.
- Pull on a rubber band. Stretch it out. Then let one end of the band go. The band snaps forward when the potential energy is changed into kinetic energy.

How do objects react to heat?

Imagine a chair made of metal. It has been out in the sunshine. If you sit on the chair, it will feel hot. Put a cloth pillow on the chair. This will make sitting in the chair comfortable.

Heat easily moves through objects called conductors. A conductor is a material that allows heat to move through it easily. Metals are heat conductors. That's why metal pots and pans are used for cooking.

Glass is not like metal. It is only a fair heat conductor. Hot water in a metal bowl makes the bowl heat up quickly. Hot water in a glass bowl just turns the inside of the bowl hot. The outside will heat up slowly.

Pots and pans are made of metal. Metal is a good conductor of heat.

Heat does not easily pass through materials called insulators. Insulators are materials that do not conduct heat well. Plastic, rubber, and wood are insulators. A cloth potholder is an insulator, too. The cloth can protect your hand because cloth doesn't conduct heat well.

Metal is a good material for pot and pans. But the handles should be made of something else. If the handles were made of metal, they would get too hot. You wouldn't be able to pick up the pot. Many pots have plastic or wood handles. These things don't conduct heat well, so they make the pot safe to handle.

Wood is an insulator. Heat does not pass through it easily. It is safe for cooks to use.

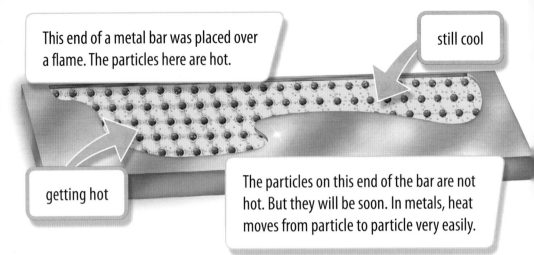

This end of a metal bar was placed over a flame. The particles here are hot.

still cool

getting hot

The particles on this end of the bar are not hot. But they will be soon. In metals, heat moves from particle to particle very easily.

How are conductors and insulators different?

Materials that conduct heat also conduct electricity. Copper is a metal. Copper wire is used to conduct electricity.

It makes sense that things that don't conduct heat also don't conduct electricity. Materials such as plastic and rubber don't conduct electricity. So, this is one way that conductors and insulators differ. Conductors allow electricity to flow, but insulators don't.

In general, solids conduct heat better than liquids or gases do. That's because the tiny pieces of a solid are packed closely. These pieces, or particles, move back and forth. But they don't move away from each other. So, heat moves quickly from one tiny piece to another.

This cat's fur will help it keep warm in cold weather. Around each thick hair is air. The air and fur both work as insulators.

Gases are good insulators. Air is a gas and it's a good insulator. How can you test this? On a cold day, wear layers of clothing when you play outside. Air will get trapped between the layers. Each thin layer of air is like a layer of insulation. These layers will keep heat close to your body.

This is another way that conductors and insulators differ. Conductors allow for the movement of heat. Insulators slow down the movement of heat.

How does an electric cord work?

Items in your home get energy from electricity. One example is a lamp. One end of an electric cord is on the lamp. The other end is plugged in to an opening in the wall called an outlet. There, the cord connects to a system of wires. These wires carry electricity. The electric cord conducts electricity to the lamp.

People can pick up the electric cord safely. What do you think makes the electric cord safe to handle?

An electric cord is made of more than one kind of material. In the center is a conductor, such as copper wire. The wire carries the electricity from the power source to the lamp. Outside the copper wire is an insulator. It might be rubber or plastic. These materials make the power cord safe to handle.

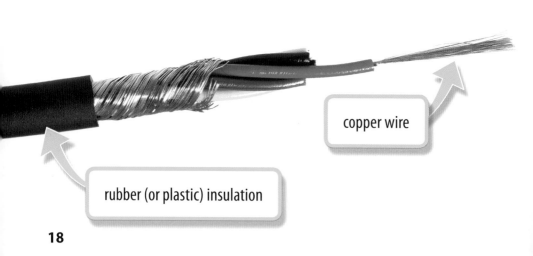

copper wire

rubber (or plastic) insulation

How does heat move and change matter?

Heat can move and change matter. One way is by conduction. Another is by convection. The third way is by radiation.

Conduction is the movement of heat between two materials that are touching. Did you ever walk barefoot on a hot summer day? Did the sidewalk feel hot? The heat from the sidewalk moved to your feet. Your body is not as hot as the sidewalk. So, the heat moved to your cooler feet.

What happens when you put a frozen juice bar in your mouth? Right away, your tongue feels cold. Soon, the heat from your mouth moves to the juice bar. The bar melts!

Heat from the hot liquid warms these hands.

This hand feels cold when it touches the iced drink. Soon, heat from the hand will warm the drink.

How do convection and radiation work?

Convection is the movement of heat within a liquid or a gas. Look at the pot of soup over the campfire. Heat moves from the burning logs to the pot. Then heat moves to the soup in the pot. The soup in the bottom of the pot gets warm. The warm soup moves up to the top of the pot. The cooler soup moves down to the bottom. There, it heats up and moves back up to the top. The heat keeps moving. It moves through the liquid in the pot.

The soup in the pot heats up because of the transfer of heat within a liquid. This process is called convection.

Light bulbs don't touch this food. But the heat from the bulbs warms it.

Radiation is the movement of heat without matter to carry it. How can that happen? Think about a winter storm. Snow and ice cover the roads. Then the sun comes out. Heat from the sun melts the snow on the roads. The sun doesn't touch the roads, but the heat does.

How can heat from the sun reach Earth through empty space? It's not conduction, because there's no matter between the sun and Earth. It's not convection, because there's no liquid or gas in space. Radiation is the reason. The heat of the sun travels to Earth by radiation.

Find the Best Insulator

With a partner, find these supplies: hot water, four glass jars, four rubber bands, aluminum foil, wax paper, plastic wrap, cotton fabric, thermometer, and a stopwatch or timer.

With an adult, pour hot water into each jar. Take the water temperature of each jar and record it in a chart. Cover the top of one jar with aluminum foil, one with wax paper, one with plastic wrap, and one with the cotton fabric. Attach the covers with a rubber band. Which material do you think will be the best insulator? Set the stopwatch for 1½ hours. Then measure the water temperature in each jar. Record the temperature. Which jar had the warmest water? Can you explain why?

Research an Energy Scientist

Work with a partner. Choose a scientist who has made contributions to the field of energy. Do research to learn more about this person. Make a poster about this person. Include pictures and words that tell why this scientist is important.

Glossary

chemical energy [KEM·ih·kuhl EN·er·jee] Energy that can be released by a chemical reaction. *Cars use chemical energy when they burn gasoline for energy.*

conduction [kuhn·DUK·shuhn] The movement of heat between two materials that are touching. *Because of conduction, you burned your mouth on hot pizza.*

conductor [kuhn·DUK·ter] A material that lets heat or electrical charges travel through it easily. *In our experiment, cotton rope was not a good conductor of electricity.*

convection [kuhn·VEK·shuhn] The transfer of heat within a liquid or gas. *A hot-air popper uses convection to make popcorn.*

electrical energy [ee·LEK·trih·kuhl EN·er·jee] Energy that comes from electric current. *A computer uses electrical energy.*

energy [EN·er·jee] The ability to cause changes in matter. *Eat well before a game because your body will need lots of energy.*

heat [HEET] The energy that moves between objects of different temperatures. *After I go sledding, the heat from the fireplace warms my hands and feet.*

insulator [IN•suh•lay•ter] A material that does not let heat or electricity move through it easily. *The wooden handles on our fireplace tools are good insulators.*

kinetic energy [kih•NET•ik EN•er•jee] The energy of motion. *Sliding, rolling, and falling are examples of kinetic energy.*

mechanical energy [muh•KAN•ih•kuhl EN•er•jee] The total potential and kinetic energy of an object. *The wagon rolling down our street has mechanical energy.*

potential energy [poh•TEN•chuhl EN•er•jee] Energy that an object has because of the object's position or its condition. *The ball has potential energy when it's still in your hand.*

radiation [ray•dee•AY•shuhn] The movement of heat without matter to carry it. *Thanks to radiation, the ice on our front steps finally melted.*

thermal energy [THUR•muhl EN•er•jee] The total kinetic energy of the particles in a substance. *A stove has thermal energy when it is turned on.*